9 5

LIFE'S LITTLE INSTRUCTION BOOK

—— ❧ ——

511 Reminders for a Happy
and Rewarding Life

H. JACKSON BROWN, Jr.

G·K·Hall&Co.

Boston, Massachusetts
1993

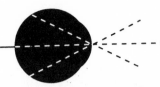

This Large Print Book carries the Seal of Approval of N.A.V.H.

Copyright © 1991 by H. Jackson Brown, Jr.

Published in Large Print by arrangement with Rutledge Hill Press, Inc.

G.K. Hall Large Print Book Series.

Printed on acid free paper in the United States of America.

Set in 18 pt. plantin.

Library of Congress Cataloging-in-Publication Data

Brown, H. Jackson, 1940–
  Life's Little instruction book : 511 reminders for a happy and rewarding life / H. Jackson Brown.
      p. cm. — (G.K. Hall large print book series)
  Originally published: Nashville, Tenn. : Rutledge Hill Press, 1991.
    ISBN 0-8161-5644-1 (alk. paper)
    1. Happiness—Quotations, maxims, etc. 2. Conduct of life—Quotations, maxims, etc. 3. Large type books. I. Title. II. Series.
BJ1481.B87 1992
170'.44—dc20   92-31115

Introduction

This book began as a gift to my son, Adam. As he packed his stereo, typewriter, blue blazer and other necessities for his new life as a college freshman, I retreated to the family room to jot down a few observations and words of counsel I thought he might find useful.

I read years ago that it was not the responsibility of parents to pave the road for their children, but to provide a road map. That's how I hoped he would use these mind and heart reflections.

I started writing, and what I thought would take a few hours took several days. I gathered my collection of handwritten notes, typed them up, and put them in a dime-store binder. I walked to the garage and slid it under the front seat of the station wagon.

A few days later his mother and I helped him move into his new dorm room. When he was all settled in, I asked him to come with me to the parking lot. It was time for the presentation. I reached under the car seat and, with words to the effect that this was what I knew about living a happy and rewarding life, handed him the bound pages. He hugged me and shook my hand. It was a very special moment.

Well, somehow those typewritten pages became the little book you're now holding. You may not agree with all the entries, and from your own life experience, I'm sure you could add hundreds more. Obviously, some are more important than others, but all have added a degree of joy, meaning, and efficiency to my life.

A few days after I had given Adam his copy, he called me from his dorm room. "Dad," he said, "I've been reading the instruction book and I think it's one of the best gifts I've ever received. I'm going to add to it and someday give it to my son."

Every once in a while life hands you a moment so precious, so overwhelming you almost glow. I know. I had just experienced one.

Son, how can I help you see?
May I give you my shoulders
   to stand on?
Now you see farther than me.
Now you see for both of us.
Won't you tell me what you see?

★★★★★★★★★★★★★★★★

1

Compliment three people every day.

2

Have a dog.

3

Watch a sunrise at least once a year.

4

Remember other people's birthdays.

5

Overtip breakfast waitresses.

★★★★★★★★★★★★★★★★

★★★★★★★★★★★★★★★★

6

Have a firm handshake.

7

Look people in the eye.

8

Say "thank you" a lot.

9

Say "please" a lot.

10

Learn to play a musical instrument.

★★★★★★★★★★★★★★★★

★★★★★★★★★★★★★★★★

11

Sing in the shower.

12

Use the good silver.

13

Learn to make great chili.

14

Plant flowers every spring.

15

Own a great stereo system.

★★★★★★★★★★★★★★★★

★★★★★★★★★★★★★★★★

16

Be the first to say, "Hello."

17

Live beneath your means.

18

Drive inexpensive cars,
but own the best house
you can afford.

19

Buy great books even if
you never read them.

★★★★★★★★★★★★★★★★

★★★★★★★★★★★★★★★★

20

Be forgiving of yourself and others.

21

Learn three clean jokes.

22

Wear polished shoes.

23

Floss your teeth.

24

Drink champagne for no reason at all.

★★★★★★★★★★★★★★★★

★★★★★★★★★★★★★★★★

25

Ask for a raise when you feel
you've earned it.

26

If in a fight, hit first and hit hard.

27

Return all things you borrow.

28

Teach some kind of class.

29

Be a student in some kind of class.

★★★★★★★★★★★★★★★★

★★★★★★★★★★★★★★★★

30

Never buy a house without a fireplace.

31

Buy whatever kids are selling
on card tables in their front yards.

32

Once in your life own a convertible.

33

Treat everyone you meet like you want
to be treated.

★★★★★★★★★★★★★★★★

★★★★★★★★★★★★★★★★

34

Learn to identify the music
of Chopin, Mozart, and Beethoven.

35

Plant a tree on your birthday.

36

Donate two pints of blood every year.

37

Make new friends but cherish
the old ones.

★★★★★★★★★★★★★★★★

★★★★★★★★★★★★★★★★

38

Keep secrets.

39

Take lots of snapshots.

40

Never refuse homemade brownies.

41

Don't postpone joy.

42

Write "thank you" notes promptly.

★★★★★★★★★★★★★★★★

★★★★★★★★★★★★★★★★

43

Never give up
on anybody.
Miracles happen every day.

★★★★★★★★★★★★★★★★

★★★★★★★★★★★★★★★★

44

Show respect for teachers.

45

Show respect for police officers
and firefighters.

46

Show respect for military personnel.

47

Don't waste time
learning the "tricks of the trade."
Instead, learn the trade.

★★★★★★★★★★★★★★★★

★★★★★★★★★★★★★★★★

48

Keep a tight rein on your temper.

49

Buy vegetables from truck farmers
who advertise with hand-lettered signs.

50

Put the cap back on the toothpaste.

51

Take out the garbage
without being told.

★★★★★★★★★★★★★★★★

★★★★★★★★★★★★★★★★

52

Avoid overexposure to the sun.

53

Vote.

54

Surprise loved ones with
little unexpected gifts.

55

Stop blaming others. Take responsibility
for every area of your life.

★★★★★★★★★★★★★★★★

★★★★★★★★★★★★★★★★

56

Never mention being on a diet.

57

Make the best of bad situations.

58

Always accept an outstretched hand.

59

Live so that when your children think of fairness, caring, and integrity, they think of you.

★★★★★★★★★★★★★★★★

★★★★★★★★★★★★★★★★

60

Admit your mistakes.

61

Ask someone to pick up your mail and daily paper when you're out of town. Those are the first two things potential burglars look for.

62

Use your wit to amuse, not abuse.

63

Remember that all news is biased.

★★★★★★★★★★★★★★★★

★★★★★★★★★★★★★★★★

64

Take a photography course.

65

Let people pull in front of you when
you're stopped in traffic.

66

Support a high school band.

67

Demand excellence and be willing
to pay for it.

★★★★★★★★★★★★★★★★

★★★★★★★★★★★★★★★★

68

Be brave.
Even if you're not,
pretend to be.
No one can tell
the difference.

★★★★★★★★★★★★★★★★

★★★★★★★★★★★★★★★★

69

Whistle.

70

Hug children after you
discipline them.

71

Learn to make something beautiful
with your hands.

72

Give to charity all the clothes you
haven't worn during the
past three years.

★★★★★★★★★★★★★★★★

★★★★★★★★★★★★★★★★

73

Never forget your anniversary.

74

Eat prunes.

75

Ride a bike.

76

Choose a charity in your community
and support it generously with
your time and money.

★★★★★★★★★★★★★★★★

77

Don't take good health for granted.

78

When someone wants to hire you,
even if it's for a job you
have little interest in,
talk to them. Never close the
door on an opportunity until you've
had a chance to hear the offer
in person.

79

Don't mess with drugs, and don't
associate with those who do.

★★★★★★★★★★★★★★★★

★★★★★★★★★★★★★★★★

80

Slow dance.

81

Avoid sarcastic remarks.

82

Steer clear of restaurants
with strolling musicians.

83

In business and in family
relationships, remember that the
most important thing is trust.

★★★★★★★★★★★★★★★★

★★★★★★★★★★★★★★★★

84

Forget the Joneses.

85

Never encourage anyone to
become a lawyer.

86

Don't smoke.

87

Even if you're financially well-to-do,
have your children earn and pay
part of their college tuition.

★★★★★★★★★★★★★★★★

★★★★★★★★★★★★★★★★

88

Even if you're financially well-to-do,
have your children earn and pay
for *all* their automobile insurance.

89

Recycle old newspapers, bottles,
and cans.

90

Refill ice cube trays.

91

Don't let anyone ever see you tipsy.

★★★★★★★★★★★★★★★★

★★★★★★★★★★★★★★★★

92

Never invest more in the stock market
than you can afford to lose.

93

Choose your life's mate carefully.
From this one decision will come
ninety percent of all your
happiness or misery.

94

Make it a habit to do nice things
for people who'll never find it out.

★★★★★★★★★★★★★★★★

★★★★★★★★★★★★★★★★

95

Attend class reunions.

96

Lend only those books
you never care to see again.

97

Always have something beautiful
in sight, even if it's just a daisy
in a jelly glass.

98

Know how to type.

★★★★★★★★★★★★★★★★

★★★★★★★★★★★★★★★★

99

Think big thoughts,
but relish small pleasures.

★★★★★★★★★★★★★★★★

★★★★★★★★★★★★★★★★

100

Read the Bill of Rights.

101

Learn how to read a financial report.

102

Tell your kids often how terrific
they are and that you trust them.

103

Use credit cards only for convenience,
never for credit.

★★★★★★★★★★★★★★★★

★★★★★★★★★★★★★★★★

104

Take a brisk thirty-minute walk
every day.

105

Treat yourself to a massage on your
birthday.

106

Never cheat.

107

Smile a lot. It costs nothing
and is beyond price.

★★★★★★★★★★★★★★★★

108

When dining with clients or
business associates,
never order more than one cocktail
or one glass of wine.
If no one else is drinking,
don't drink at all.

109

Know how to drive a stick shift.

110

Spread crunchy peanut butter
on Pepperidge Farm Gingerman
cookies for the perfect
late-night snack.

★★★★★★★★★★★★★★★★

★★★★★★★★★★★★★★★★

111

Never use profanity.

112

Never argue with police officers,
and address them as "officer."

113

Learn to identify local
wildflowers, birds, and trees.

114

Keep a fire extinguisher in your
kitchen and car.

★★★★★★★★★★★★★★★★

★★★★★★★★★★★★★★★★

115

Give yourself a year and read
the Bible cover to cover.

116

Consider writing a living will.

117

Install dead bolt locks
on outside doors.

118

Don't buy expensive wine, luggage,
or watches.

★★★★★★★★★★★★★★★★

★★★★★★★★★★★★★★★★

119

Put a lot of little marshmallows
in your hot chocolate.

120

Learn CPR.

121

Resist the temptation to buy a boat.

122

Stop and read historical
roadside markers.

★★★★★★★★★★★★★★★★

★★★★★★★★★★★★★★★★

123

Learn to listen.
Opportunity
sometimes knocks
very softly.

★★★★★★★★★★★★★★★★

★★★★★★★★★★★★★★★★

124

Know how to change a tire.

125

Know how to tie a bow tie.

126

Respect your children's privacy.
Knock before entering their room.

127

Wear audacious underwear
under the most solemn
business attire.

★★★★★★★★★★★★★★★★

★★★★★★★★★★★★★★★★

128

Remember people's names.

129

Introduce yourself to the manager
where you bank. It's important that
he/she knows you personally.

130

Leave the toilet seat in the
down position.

131

Learn the capitals of the states.

★★★★★★★★★★★★★★★★

132

Visit Washington, D.C., and
do the tourist bit.

133

When someone is relating an
important event that's happened
to them, don't try to top them
with a story of your own.
Let them have the stage.

134

Don't buy cheap tools.
Craftsman tools from Sears are
among the best.

★★★★★★★★★★★★★★★★

★★★★★★★★★★★★★★★★

135

Have crooked teeth straightened.

136

Have dull-colored teeth whitened.

137

Keep your watch five minutes fast.

138

Learn Spanish. In a few years, more than thirty-five percent of all Americans will speak it as their first language.

★★★★★★★★★★★★★★★★

★★★★★★★★★★★★★★★★
139

Never deprive
someone of hope;
it might be all they have.

★★★★★★★★★★★★★★★★

★★★★★★★★★★★★★★★★

140

When starting out, don't worry
about not having enough money.
Limited funds are a blessing,
not a curse. Nothing encourages
creative thinking in quite
the same way.

141

Give yourself an hour to cool
off before responding to someone
who has provoked you.
If it involves something really
important, give yourself overnight.

★★★★★★★★★★★★★★★★

★★★★★★★★★★★★★★★★

142

Pay your bills on time.

143

Join a slow-pitch softball league.

144

Take someone bowling.

145

Keep a flashlight and extra batteries under the bed and in the glove box of your car.

★★★★★★★★★★★★★★★★

146

When playing games with children,
let them win.

147

Turn off the television at dinner time.

148

Learn to handle a pistol and rifle safely.

149

Skip one meal a week and give
what you would have spent to a
street person.

★★★★★★★★★★★★★★★★

★★★★★★★★★★★★★★★★

150

Sing in a choir.

151

Get acquainted with a good
lawyer, accountant, and plumber.

152

Fly Old Glory on the Fourth of July.

153

Stand at attention and put your
hand over your heart when singing
the national anthem.

★★★★★★★★★★★★★★★★

★★★★★★★★★★★★★★★★

154

Resist the temptation to put a cute message on your answering machine.

155

Have a will and tell your next-of-kin where it is.

156

Strive for excellence, not perfection.

157

Take time to smell the roses.

★★★★★★★★★★★★★★★★

★★★★★★★★★★★★★★★★

158

Pray not for things,
but for wisdom and courage.

159

Be tough minded but tenderhearted.

160

Use seat belts.

161

Have regular medical and
dental checkups.

★★★★★★★★★★★★★★★★

★★★★★★★★★★★★★★★★

162

Keep your desk and work area neat.

163

Take an overnight train trip
and sleep in a Pullman.

164

Be punctual and insist on it in others.

165

Don't waste time responding
to your critics.

★★★★★★★★★★★★★★★★

★★★★★★★★★★★★★★★★

166

Avoid negative people.

167

Don't scrimp in order to
leave money to your children.

168

Resist telling people how something
should be done. Instead, tell them
what needs to be done.
They will often surprise you
with creative solutions.

★★★★★★★★★★★★★★★★

★★★★★★★★★★★★★★★★

169

Be original.

170

Be neat.

171

Never give up on what you really
want to do. The person with big
dreams is more powerful
than one with all the facts.

172

Be suspicious of all politicians.

★★★★★★★★★★★★★★★★

★★★★★★★★★★★★★★★★

173

Be kinder
than necessary.

★★★★★★★★★★★★★★★★

★★★★★★★★★★★★★★★★

174

Encourage your children to have
a part-time job after the age of sixteen.

175

Give people a second chance,
but not a third.

176

Read carefully anything
that requires your signature.
Remember the big print giveth
and the small print taketh away.

★★★★★★★★★★★★★★★★

★★★★★★★★★★★★★★★★

177

Never take action when you're angry.

178

Learn to recognize the inconsequential, then ignore it.

179

Be your wife's best friend.

180

Do battle against prejudice and discrimination wherever you find it.

★★★★★★★★★★★★★★★★

★★★★★★★★★★★★★★★★

181

Wear out, don't rust out.

182

Be romantic.

183

Let people know what you stand for—
and what you won't stand for.

184

Don't quit a job
until you've lined up another.

★★★★★★★★★★★★★★★★

★★★★★★★★★★★★★★★★

185

Never criticize the person
who signs your paycheck.
If you are unhappy with your job,
resign.

186

Be insatiably curious.
Ask "why" a lot.

187

Measure people by the size
of their hearts,
not the size of their bank accounts.

★★★★★★★★★★★★★★★★

★★★★★★★★★★★★★★★★

188

Become the most positive
and enthusiastic person
you know.

★★★★★★★★★★★★★★★★

★★★★★★★★★★★★★★★★

189

Learn how to fix a leaky faucet
and toilet.

190

Have good posture.
Enter a room with purpose
and confidence.

191

Don't worry that you can't
give your kids the best of everything.
Give them *your* very best.

★★★★★★★★★★★★★★★★

★★★★★★★★★★★★★★★★

192

Drink low fat milk.

193

Use less salt.

194

Eat less red meat.

195

Determine the quality of a
neighborhood by the manners
of the people living there.

★★★★★★★★★★★★★★★★

★★★★★★★★★★★★★★★★

196

Surprise a new neighbor
with one of your favorite homemade
dishes—and include the recipe.

197

Don't forget,
a person's greatest emotional need
is to feel appreciated.

198

Feed a stranger's expired parking meter.

★★★★★★★★★★★★★★★★

★★★★★★★★★★★★★★★★

199

Park at the back of the lot
at shopping centers.
The walk is good exercise.

200

Don't watch violent television
shows, and don't buy the products
that sponsor them.

201

Don't carry a grudge.

202

Show respect for all living things.

★★★★★★★★★★★★★★★★

★★★★★★★★★★★★★★★★

203

Return borrowed vehicles
with the gas tank full.

204

Choose work that is
in harmony with your values.

205

Loosen up. Relax. Except for
rare life-and-death matters, nothing
is as important as it first seems.

★★★★★★★★★★★★★★★★

★★★★★★★★★★★★★★★★

206

Give your best to your employer.
It's one of the best investments
you can make.

207

Swing for the fence.

208

Attend high school art shows,
and always buy something.

209

Observe the speed limit.

★★★★★★★★★★★★★★★★

★★★★★★★★★★★★★★★★

210

Commit yourself
to constant
self-improvement.

★★★★★★★★★★★★★★★★

★★★★★★★★★★★★★★★★

211

Take your dog to obedience school.
You'll both learn a lot.

212

Don't allow the phone
to interrupt important moments.
It's there for your convenience,
not the caller's.

213

Don't waste time grieving over
past mistakes. Learn from
them and move on.

★★★★★★★★★★★★★★★★

★★★★★★★★★★★★★★★★

214

When complimented, a sincere
"thank you"
is the only response required.

215

Don't plan a long evening on
a blind date. A lunch date is perfect.
If things don't work out, both of you
have only wasted an hour.

216

Don't discuss business in elevators.
You never know who may overhear you.

★★★★★★★★★★★★★★★★

★★★★★★★★★★★★★★★★

217

Be a good loser.

218

Be a good winner.

219

Never go grocery shopping when
you're hungry.
You'll buy too much.

220

Spend less time worrying *who's* right,
and more time deciding *what's* right.

★★★★★★★★★★★★★★★★

★★★★★★★★★★★★★★★★

221

Don't major
in minor things.

★★★★★★★★★★★★★★★★

★★★★★★★★★★★★★★★★

222

Think twice before burdening
a friend with a secret.

223

Praise in public.

224

Criticize in private.

225

Never tell anyone they look
tired or depressed.

★★★★★★★★★★★★★★★★

★★★★★★★★★★★★★★★★

226

When someone hugs you,
let them be the first to let go.

227

Resist giving advice concerning,
matrimony, finances, or hair styles.

228

Have impeccable manners.

229

Never pay for work before
it's completed.

★★★★★★★★★★★★★★★★

★★★★★★★★★★★★★★★★

230

Keep good company.

231

Keep a daily journal.

232

Keep your promises.

233

Avoid any church that has cushions
on the pews and is considering
building a gymnasium.

★★★★★★★★★★★★★★★★

★★★★★★★★★★★★★★★★

234

Teach your children the value of money
and the importance of saving.

235

Be willing to lose a battle
in order to win the war.

236

Don't be deceived by first impressions.

237

Seek out the good in people.

★★★★★★★★★★★★★★★★

★★★★★★★★★★★★★★★★

238

Don't encourage rude or inattentive
service by tipping the
standard amount.

239

Watch the movie
It's A Wonderful Life every Christmas.

240

Drink eight glasses of water every day.

241

Respect tradition.

★★★★★★★★★★★★★★★★

★★★★★★★★★★★★★★★★

242

Be cautious about lending
money to friends.
You might lose both.

243

Never waste an opportunity
to tell good employees how much
they mean to the company.

244

Buy a bird feeder and hang it
so that you can see it from
your kitchen window.

★★★★★★★★★★★★★★★★

★★★★★★★★★★★★★★★★

245

Never cut
what can be untied.

★★★★★★★★★★★★★★★★

★★★★★★★★★★★★★★★★

246

Wave at children on school buses.

247

Tape record your parents' memories
of how they met and their first
years of marriage.

248

Show respect for others' time.
Call whenever you're going to be
more than ten minutes late
for an appointment.

★★★★★★★★★★★★★★★★

★★★★★★★★★★★★★★★★

249

Hire people smarter than you.

250

Learn to show cheerfulness,
even when you don't feel like it.

251

Learn to show enthusiasm,
even when you don't feel like it.

252

Take good care of those you love.

★★★★★★★★★★★★★★★★

★★★★★★★★★★★★★★★★

253

Be modest. A lot was accomplished before you were born.

254

Keep it simple.

255

Purchase gas from the neighborhood gas station even if it costs more. Next winter when it's six degrees and your car won't start, you'll be glad they know you.

★★★★★★★★★★★★★★★★

★★★★★★★★★★★★★★★★

256

Don't jaywalk.

257

Never ask a lawyer or accountant for business advice. They are trained to find problems, not solutions.

258

When meeting someone for the first time, resist asking what they do for a living. Enjoy their company without attaching any labels.

★★★★★★★★★★★★★★★★

★★★★★★★★★★★★★★★★

259

Avoid like the plague any lawsuit.

260

Every day show your family how much you love them with your words, with your touch, and with your thoughtfulness.

261

Take family vacations whether you can afford them or not. The memories will be priceless.

★★★★★★★★★★★★★★★★

★★★★★★★★★★★★★★★★

262

Don't gossip.

263

Don't discuss salaries.

264

Don't nag.

265

Don't gamble.

266

Beware of the person who has nothing to lose.

★★★★★★★★★★★★★★★★

★★★★★★★★★★★★★★★★

267

Lie on your back and look at the stars.

268

Don't leave car keys in the ignition.

269

Don't whine.

270

Arrive at work early
and stay beyond quitting time.

★★★★★★★★★★★★★★★★

★★★★★★★★★★★★★★★★

271

When facing a difficult task,
act as though it is impossible to fail.
If you're going after Moby Dick,
take along the tarter sauce.

272

Change air conditioner filters
every three months.

273

Remember that overnight success
usually takes about fifteen years.

★★★★★★★★★★★★★★★★

★★★★★★★★★★★★★★★★

274

Leave everything
a little better
than you found it.

★★★★★★★★★★★★★★★★

★★★★★★★★★★★★★★★★

275

Cut out complimentary newspaper
articles about people you know
and mail the articles to them with
notes of congratulations.

276

Patronize local merchants
even if it costs a bit more.

277

Fill your gas tank when it falls
below one-quarter full.

★★★★★★★★★★★★★★★★

★★★★★★★★★★★★★★★★

278

Don't expect money to
bring you happiness.

279

Never snap your fingers to get
someone's attention. It's rude.

280

No matter how dire the situation,
keep your cool.

281

When paying cash, ask for a discount.

★★★★★★★★★★★★★★★★

★★★★★★★★★★★★★★★★

282

Find a good tailor.

283

Don't use a toothpick in public.

284

Never underestimate
your power to change yourself.

285

Never overestimate your power
to change others.

★★★★★★★★★★★★★★★★

★★★★★★★★★★★★★★★★

286

Practice empathy. Try to see things from other people's point of view.

287

Promise big. Deliver big.

288

Discipline yourself to save money. It's essential to success.

289

Get and stay in shape.

★★★★★★★★★★★★★★★★

290

Find some other way of proving
your manhood than by
shooting defenseless animals
and birds.

291

Remember the deal's not done
until the check has cleared the bank.

292

Don't burn bridges. You'll be surprised
how many times you have to cross
the same river.

★★★★★★★★★★★★★★★★

★★★★★★★★★★★★★★★★

293

Don't spread yourself too thin.
Learn to say *no* politely and quickly.

294

Keep overhead low.

295

Keep expectations high.

296

Accept pain and disappointment
as part of life.

★★★★★★★★★★★★★★★★

★★★★★★★★★★★★★★★★

297

Remember that a successful marriage
depends on two things:
(1) finding the right person and
(2) being the right person.

298

See problems as opportunities
for growth and self-mastery.

299

Don't believe people when
they ask you to be honest
with them.

★★★★★★★★★★★★★★★★

★★★★★★★★★★★★★★★★

300

Don't expect life to be fair.

301

Become an expert in time management.

302

Lock your car even if it's
parked in your own driveway.

303

Never go to bed with dirty dishes
in the sink.

★★★★★★★★★★★★★★★★

★★★★★★★★★★★★★★★★

304

Judge your success
by the degree
that you're enjoying
peace, health, and love.

★★★★★★★★★★★★★★★★

305

Learn to handle a handsaw
and a hammer.

306

Take a nap on Sunday afternoons.

307

Compliment the meal when you're
a guest in someone's home.

308

Make the bed when you're an
overnight visitor in someone's home.

★★★★★★★★★★★★★★★★

★★★★★★★★★★★★★★★★

309

Contribute five percent of your
income to charity.

310

Don't leave a ring in the bathtub.

311

Don't waste time playing cards.

312

When tempted to criticize
your parents,
spouse, or children,
bite your tongue.

★★★★★★★★★★★★★★★★

★★★★★★★★★★★★★★★★

313

Never underestimate the power of love.

314

Never underestimate the power
of forgiveness.

315

Don't bore people with your
problems. When someone asks you how
you feel—say, "Terrific, never better."
When they ask, "How's business?"
reply, "Excellent, and getting better
every day."

★★★★★★★★★★★★★★★★

★★★★★★★★★★★★★★★★

316

Learn to disagree
without being disagreeable.

317

Be tactful. Never alienate
anyone on purpose.

318

Hear both sides before judging.

319

Refrain from envy.
It's the source of much unhappiness.

★★★★★★★★★★★★★★★★

★★★★★★★★★★★★★★★★

320

Be courteous to everyone.

321

Wave to crosswalk patrol mothers.

322

Don't say you don't have
enough time. You have exactly
the same number of hours per day
that were given to Pasteur,
Michaelangelo, Mother Teresa,
Helen Keller, Leonardo da Vinci,
Thomas Jefferson, and Albert Einstein.

★★★★★★★★★★★★★★★★

★★★★★★★★★★★★★★★★

323

When there's no time for a
full work-out, do push-ups.

324

Don't delay acting on a good idea.
Chances are someone else has just
thought of it, too. Success comes to
the one who acts first.

325

Be wary of people who tell you
how honest they are.

★★★★★★★★★★★★★★★★

★★★★★★★★★★★★★★★★

326

Remember that winners do
what losers don't want to do.

327

When you arrive at your job in
the morning, let the first thing you say
brighten everyone's day.

328

Seek opportunity, not security.
A boat in a harbor is safe, but
in time its bottom will rot out.

★★★★★★★★★★★★★★★★

★★★★★★★★★★★★★★★★

329

Install smoke detectors in your home.

330

Rekindle old friendships.

331

When traveling, put a card in
your wallet with your name,
home phone, the phone
number of a friend or close relative,
important medical information,
plus the phone number of the
hotel or motel where you're staying.

★★★★★★★★★★★★★★★★

★★★★★★★★★★★★★★★★

332

Live your life as
an exclamation,
not an explanation.

★★★★★★★★★★★★★★★★

★★★★★★★★★★★★★★★★

333

Instead of using the words, *if only,*
try substituting the words, *next time.*

334

Instead of using the word *problem,*
try substituting the word *opportunity.*

335

Ever so often push your luck.

336

Get your next pet from the
animal shelter.

★★★★★★★★★★★★★★★★

★★★★★★★★★★★★★★★★

337

Reread your favorite book.

338

Live your life so that your
epitaph could read, "No regrets."

339

Never walk out on a quarrel
with your wife.

340

Don't think a higher price
always means higher quality.

★★★★★★★★★★★★★★★★

★★★★★★★★★★★★★★★★

341

Don't be fooled. If something sounds too good to be true, it probably is.

342

When renting a car for a couple of days, splurge and get the big Lincoln.

343

Regarding furniture and clothes: if you think you'll be using them five years or longer, buy the best you can afford.

★★★★★★★★★★★★★★★★

★★★★★★★★★★★★★★★★

344

Patronize drug stores with
soda fountains.

345

Try everything offered by
supermarket food demonstrators.

346

Be bold and courageous.
When you look back on your life,
you'll regret the things you didn't do
more than the ones you did.

★★★★★★★★★★★★★★★★

★★★★★★★★★★★★★★★★

347

Never waste
an opportunity to tell
someone you love them.

★★★★★★★★★★★★★★★★

★★★★★★★★★★★★★★★★

348

Own a good dictionary.

349

Own a good thesaurus.

350

Remember the three most important things when buying a home: location, location, location.

351

Keep valuable papers in a bank lockbox.

★★★★★★★★★★★★★★★★

★★★★★★★★★★★★★★★★

352

Just for fun, attend a small town
Fourth of July celebration.

353

Go through all your old
photographs. Select ten and tape
them to your kitchen cabinets.
Change them every thirty days.

354

To explain a romantic break-up,
simply say, "It was all my fault."

★★★★★★★★★★★★★★★★

★★★★★★★★★★★★★★★★

355

Evaluate yourself by your own
standards, not someone else's.

356

Be there when people need you.

357

Let your representatives in
Washington know how you feel.
Call (202) 225-3121 for the House
and (202) 224-3121 for the Senate.
An operator will connect you to
the right office.

★★★★★★★★★★★★★★★★

★★★★★★★★★★★★★★★★

358

Be decisive even if it means
you'll sometimes be wrong.

359

Don't let anyone talk you out
of pursuing what you know to be
a great idea.

360

Be prepared to lose once in a while.

361

Never eat the last cookie.

★★★★★★★★★★★★★★★★

★★★★★★★★★★★★★★★★

362

Know when to keep silent.

363

Know when to speak up.

364

Every day look for some small way
to improve your marriage.

365

Every day look for some small way
to improve the way you do your job.

★★★★★★★★★★★★★★★★

★★★★★★★★★★★★★★★★

366

Don't flush urinals with
your hand—use your elbow.

367

Acquire things the old-fashioned way:
Save for them and pay cash.

368

Remember no one makes it alone.
Have a grateful heart and be quick
to acknowledge those who help you.

★★★★★★★★★★★★★★★★

★★★★★★★★★★★★★★★★

369

Read *Leadership is an Art* by
Max DePree
(Dell, 1989).

370

Do business with those
who do business with you.

371

Just to see how it feels,
for the next twenty-four hours
refrain from criticizing anybody
or anything.

★★★★★★★★★★★★★★★★

★★★★★★★★★★★★★★★★

372

Give your clients your enthusiastic best.

373

Let your children overhear you
saying complimentary things
about them to other adults.

374

Work hard to create in your children
a good self-image. It's the most
important thing you can do to
insure their success.

★★★★★★★★★★★★★★★★

★★★★★★★★★★★★★★★★

375

Take charge
of your attitude.
Don't let someone else
choose it for you.

★★★★★★★★★★★★★★★★

★★★★★★★★★★★★★★★★

376

Save an evening a week
for just you and your wife.

377

Carry jumper cables in your car.

378

Get all repair estimates in writing.

379

Forget committees. New,
noble, world-changing ideas
always come from one person
working alone.

★★★★★★★★★★★★★★★★

★★★★★★★★★★★★★★★★

380

Pay attention to the details.

381

Be a self-starter.

382

Be loyal.

383

Understand that happiness is not
based on possessions, power, or
prestige, but on relationships
with people you love
and respect.

★★★★★★★★★★★★★★★★

★★★★★★★★★★★★★★★★

384

Never give a loved one a gift that suggests they need improvement.

385

Compliment even small improvements.

386

Turn off the tap when brushing your teeth.

387

Wear expensive shoes, belts, and ties, but buy them on sale.

★★★★★★★★★★★★★★★★

★★★★★★★★★★★★★★★★

388

When undecided about
what color to paint a room,
choose antique white.

389

Carry stamps in your wallet.
You never know when you'll
discover the perfect card for a
friend or loved one.

390

Street musicians are a treasure.
Stop for a moment and listen;
then leave a small donation.

★★★★★★★★★★★★★★★★

★★★★★★★★★★★★★★★★

391

Support equal pay for equal work.

392

Pay your fair share.

393

Learn how to operate a
Macintosh computer.

394

When faced with a serious health
problem, get at least three
medical opinions.

★★★★★★★★★★★★★★★★

★★★★★★★★★★★★★★★★

395

Remain open, flexible, curious.

396

Never give anyone a fruitcake.

397

Never acquire just one kitten.
Two are a lot more fun and
no more trouble.

398

Start meetings on time
regardless of who's missing.

★★★★★★★★★★★★★★★★

★★★★★★★★★★★★★★★★

399

Focus on
making things better,
not bigger.

★★★★★★★★★★★★★★★★

★★★★★★★★★★★★★★★★

400

Stay out of nightclubs.

401

Don't ever watch hot dogs
or sausage being made.

402

Begin each day with your
favorite music.

403

Visit your city's night court
on a Saturday night.

★★★★★★★★★★★★★★★★

★★★★★★★★★★★★★★★★

404

When attending meetings,
sit down front.

405

Don't be intimidated by doctors
and nurses. Even when you're
in the hospital,
it's still your body.

406

Read hospital bills carefully.
It's reported that 89% contain errors
—in favor of the hospital.

★★★★★★★★★★★★★★★★

★★★★★★★★★★★★★★★★

407

Every once in a while,
take the scenic route.

408

Don't let your possessions possess you.

409

Wage war against littering.

410

Send a lot of Valentine cards.
Sign them, "Someone who thinks
you're terrific."

★★★★★★★★★★★★★★★★

★★★★★★★★★★★★★★★★

411

Cut your own firewood.

412

When you and your wife have
a disagreement, regardless of
who's wrong, apologize. Say,
"I'm sorry I upset you.
Would you forgive me?"
These are healing, magical words.

413

Don't flaunt your success,
but don't apologize for it either.

★★★★★★★★★★★★★★★★

★★★★★★★★★★★★★★★★

414

After experiencing inferior service,
food, or products, bring it to the
attention of the person in charge.
Good managers will
appreciate knowing.

415

Be enthusiastic about the success
of others.

416

Don't procrastinate. Do what needs
doing when it needs to be done.

★★★★★★★★★★★★★★★★

★★★★★★★★★★★★★★★★

417

Read to your children.

418

Sing to your children.

419

Listen to your children.

420

Get your priorities straight.
No one ever said on his death bed,
"Gee, if I'd only spent more time
at the office."

★★★★★★★★★★★★★★★★

★★★★★★★★★★★★★★★★

421

Take care
of your reputation.
It's your
most valuable asset.

★★★★★★★★★★★★★★★★

★★★★★★★★★★★★★★★★

422

Turn on your headlights when it
begins to rain.

423

Don't tailgate.

424

Sign and carry your organ donor card.

425

Don't allow self-pity.
The moment this emotion strikes,
do something nice for someone
less fortunate than you.

★★★★★★★★★★★★★★★★

★★★★★★★★★★★★★★★★

426

Share the credit.

427

Don't accept "good enough" as good enough.

428

Do more than is expected.

429

Go to a county fair and check out the 4-H Club exhibits. It will renew your faith in the younger generation.

★★★★★★★★★★★★★★★★

★★★★★★★★★★★★★★★★

430

Select a doctor your own age
so that you can grow old together.

431

Use club soda as an
emergency spot remover.

432

Improve your performance
by improving your attitude.

433

Have a friend who owns a truck.

★★★★★★★★★★★★★★★★

★★★★★★★★★★★★★★★★

434

At the movies, buy Junior Mints
and sprinkle them on your popcorn.

435

Make a list of twenty-five things
you want to experience before you die.
Carry it in your wallet and
refer to it often.

436

Have some knowledge of
three religions other than your own.

★★★★★★★★★★★★★★★★

437

Answer the phone with enthusiasm
and energy in your voice.

438

Every person that you meet knows
something you don't; learn from them.

439

Tape record your parents' laughter.

440

Buy cars that have air bags.

★★★★★★★★★★★★★★★★

★★★★★★★★★★★★★★★★

441

When meeting someone you
don't know well,
extend your hand and give them
your name. Never assume they
remember you even if you've
met them before.

442

Do it right the first time.

443

Laugh a lot.
A good sense of humor cures
almost all of life's ills.

★★★★★★★★★★★★★★★★

★★★★★★★★★★★★★★★★

444

Never underestimate
the power
of a kind word or deed.

★★★★★★★★★★★★★★★★

445

Don't undertip the waiter just
because the food is bad;
he didn't cook it.

446

Change your car's oil and filter
every three thousand miles
regardless of what the
owner's manual recommends.

447

Conduct family fire drills.
Be sure everyone knows what to do
in case the house catches fire.

★★★★★★★★★★★★★★★★

★★★★★★★★★★★★★★★★

448

Don't be afraid to say,
"I don't know."

449

Don't be afraid to say,
"I made a mistake."

450

Don't be afraid to say,
"I need help."

451

Don't be afraid to say,
"I'm sorry."

452

Never compromise your integrity.

★★★★★★★★★★★★★★★★

453

Keep a note pad and pencil
on your bedside table.
Million-dollar ideas sometimes
strike at 3 A.M.

454

Show respect for everyone who works
for a living, regardless of how trivial
their job.

455

Read the Sunday *New York Times*
to keep informed.

★★★★★★★★★★★★★★★★

456

Send your loved one flowers.
Think of a reason later.

457

Attend your children's
athletic contests, plays, and recitals.

458

When you find a job that's ideal,
take it regardless of the pay.
If you've got what it takes,
your salary will soon reflect
your value to the company.

★★★★★★★★★★★★★★★★

★★★★★★★★★★★★★★★★

459

Don't use time or words
carelessly.
Neither can be retrieved.

★★★★★★★★★★★★★★★★

★★★★★★★★★★★★★★★★

460

Look for opportunities
to make people feel important.

461

Get organized. If you don't
know where to start, read
Stephanie Winston's
Getting Organized
(Warner Books, 1978).

462

When a child falls and skins
a knee or elbow,
always show concern; then take the
time to "kiss it and make it well."

★★★★★★★★★★★★★★★★

★★★★★★★★★★★★★★★★

463

Be open to new ideas.

464

Don't miss the magic of the moment by focusing on what's to come.

465

When talking to the press, remember they always have the last word.

466

Set short-term and long-term goals.

★★★★★★★★★★★★★★★★

★★★★★★★★★★★★★★★★

467

When planning a trip abroad,
read about the places you'll visit
before you go or, better yet,
rent a travel video.

468

Don't rain on other people's parades.

469

Stand when greeting a visitor
to your office.

470

Don't interrupt.

★★★★★★★★★★★★★★★★

★★★★★★★★★★★★★★★★

471

Before leaving to meet a flight,
call the airline first to be sure
it's on time.

472

Enjoy real maple syrup.

473

Don't be rushed into making an
important decision. People will
understand if you say, "I'd like a little
more time to think it over.
Can I get back to you tomorrow?"

★★★★★★★★★★★★★★★★

★★★★★★★★★★★★★★★★

474

Be prepared. You never get a
second chance to make a good
first impression.

475

Don't expect others to listen to
your advice and ignore
your example.

476

Go the distance.
When you accept a task,
finish it.

★★★★★★★★★★★★★★★★

★★★★★★★★★★★★★★★★

477

Give thanks before every meal.

478

Don't insist on running someone
else's life.

479

Respond promptly to R.S.V.P.
invitations. If there's a
phone number, call;
if not, write a note.

480

Take a kid to the zoo.

★★★★★★★★★★★★★★★★

★★★★★★★★★★★★★★★★

481

Watch for big problems.
They disguise
big opportunities.

★★★★★★★★★★★★★★★★

★★★★★★★★★★★★★★★★

482

Get into the habit of putting
your billfold and car keys
in the same place when entering
your home.

483

Learn a card trick.

484

Steer clear of restaurants that rotate.

485

Give people the benefit of the doubt.

★★★★★★★★★★★★★★★★

★★★★★★★★★★★★★★★★

486

Never admit at work
that you're tired, angry, or bored.

487

Decide to get up thirty minutes
earlier. Do this for a year,
and you will add seven and one-half
days to your waking world.

488

Make someone's day by paying the toll
for the person in the car behind you.

★★★★★★★★★★★★★★★★

★★★★★★★★★★★★★★★★★

489

Don't make the same mistake twice.

490

Don't drive on slick tires.

491

Keep an extra key hidden somewhere
on your car in case you
lock yourself out.

492

Put an insulation blanket around your
hot water heater to conserve energy.

★★★★★★★★★★★★★★★★

★★★★★★★★★★★★★★★★

493

Save ten percent of what you earn.

494

Never discuss money with
people who have much more
or much less than you.

495

Never buy a beige car.

496

Never buy something you don't need
just because it's on sale.

★★★★★★★★★★★★★★★★

★★★★★★★★★★★★★★★★

497

Don't be called out on strikes.
Go down swinging.

★★★★★★★★★★★★★★★★

★★★★★★★★★★★★★★★★

498

Question your goals by asking,
"Will this help me become
my very best?"

499

Cherish your children for
what they are,
not for what you'd like them to be.

500

When negotiating your salary,
think of what you want; then ask
for ten percent more.

★★★★★★★★★★★★★★★★

★★★★★★★★★★★★★★★★

501

Keep several irons in the fire.

502

After you've worked hard to get
what you want,
take the time to enjoy it.

503

Be alert for opportunities
to show praise and appreciation.

504

Commit yourself to quality.

★★★★★★★★★★★★★★★★

★★★★★★★★★★★★★★★★

505

Be a leader:
Remember the lead sled dog
is the only one with a decent view.

506

Never underestimate the
power of words to heal and
reconcile relationships.

507

Your mind can only hold
one thought at a time.
Make it a positive and constructive one.

★★★★★★★★★★★★★★★★

★★★★★★★★★★★★★★★★

508

Become someone's hero.

509

Marry only for love.

510

Count your blessings.

511

Call your mother.

★★★★★★★★★★★★★★★★